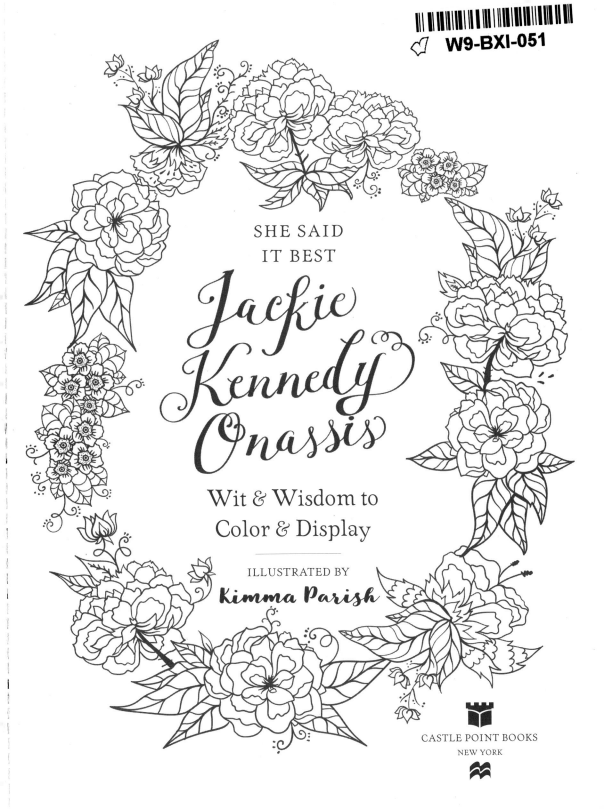

SHE SAID
IT BEST

Jackie Kennedy Onassis

Wit & Wisdom to
Color & Display

ILLUSTRATED BY
Kimma Parish

CASTLE POINT BOOKS
NEW YORK

Introduction

JACQUELINE KENNEDY ONASSIS (July 28, 1929 – May 19, 1994) is one of the most beloved and respected figures in American history. The personification of elegance, sophistication, and tenacity, Jackie is most widely known as the First Lady of the United States during John F. Kennedy's presidency until his assassination in 1963. Jackie transformed a once passive role in the White House to a position of action—she was devoted to history and the arts, spearheading the restoration of the White House to become an emblematic site of American history. She continuously supported writers, musicians, and artists during the era of "Camelot," and later thrived in a successful career as a book editor in New York over the course of two decades.

Remembered too as a fashion icon—from her infamous pink Chanel suit to her timeless sunglasses, she was a model of poise and a fiercely devoted mother who became a symbol of resilience and strength. Her poignant and practical advice on independence, womanhood, and family continues to have an impact across generations. In *She Said It Best: Jackie Kennedy Onassis*, you'll find gorgeous pages of hand-drawn art that honor the 35th First Lady's eloquent words and insights.

SHE SAID IT BEST is a celebration of the women who have shown us life in vibrant color. From famous authors and musicians to philanthropists and socialites, these women are the voices of many generations, each of whom has written, spoken, or sung wisdom into our lives. Whether it's mending a broken heart, standing up for a cause, or adding some class—and maybe some sass—to any situation, the advice and witticisms from these beloved women continue to inspire, encourage, and empower.

This unique coloring book series captures the insight, beauty, and timelessness of these leading women—from Dolly Parton to Jane Austin—with some of their most memorable and distinguished words. Hand-drawn illustrations adorn each saying and convey the unique charm and spirit that made them extraordinary. Decorate the pages of *She Said It Best* in honor of the woman on the cover, or to fill your world with a little more love, light, and wisdom.

You have to be doing something you enjoy.
That is a definition of happiness: Complete use
of one's faculties along lines leading to
excellence in a life affording them scope.

I think my biggest
achievement is that,
after going through
a rather difficult time,
I consider myself
comparatively sane.

You have only one chance to raise your child.

We should all do something, to right the wrongs that we see & not just complain about them.

I don't like to hear people say that I am poised and maintaining a good appearance. I am not a movie actress.

It's rather hard to stop once the floodgates open.

The one thing I do not want to be called
is First Lady. It sounds like a saddle horse.

The good, the bad, hardship, the joy,
the tragedy, love, and happiness
are all interwoven into one single,
indescribable whole that is called life.

The first time you marry for love, the second
for money, and the third for companionship.

If school days are the happiest days of your life,
I'm hanging myself with my skip-rope tonight.

The only routine with me is no routine at all.

YOU ARE ABOUT TO HAVE YOUR FIRST
EXPERIENCE WITH A GREEK LUNCH. I WILL
KILL YOU IF YOU PRETEND TO LIKE IT.

I am a woman above
everything else.

I want minimum information given with maximum politeness.

War might be started not so much by the big men
as by the little ones…moved more by fear and pride.

A newspaper reported I spend $30,000 a year buying Paris clothes and that women hate me for it. I couldn't spend that much unless I wore sable underwear.

Whenever I was upset by something in the papers,
Jack always told me to be more tolerant,
like a horse flicking away flies in the summer.

What is sad for women of my generation is that they weren't supposed to work if they had families. What were they going to do when the children are grown—watch the raindrops coming down the window pane?

One should always dress like
a marble column.

I came home glad to start...again but with a love
for Europe that I am afraid will never leave me.

PEARLS
ARE ALWAYS
APPROPRIATE.

There are many little ways to
enlarge your child's world.
Love of books is the best of all.

I don't really want to sit at a window looking
out at a field and feel that life is going by.

There will be great
presidents again
but there will
never be another
Camelot.

You cannot separate the good from the bad.
And perhaps there is no need to do so, either.

Being a reporter
seems a ticket
out to the
world.

Sex is a bad thing because it rumples the clothes.

When Harvard men say they have graduated
from Radcliffe, then we've made it.

If [children]
are not inspired
by the past of our
city, where will
they find the
strength to fight
for her future?

The trouble
with me is
that I'm an
outsider.
And that's
a very hard
thing to be in
American life.

I've always thought of being in love as being willing
to do anything for the other person—starve to buy them
bread and not mind living in Siberia with them.

...I think I should
have known that he was
magic all along.

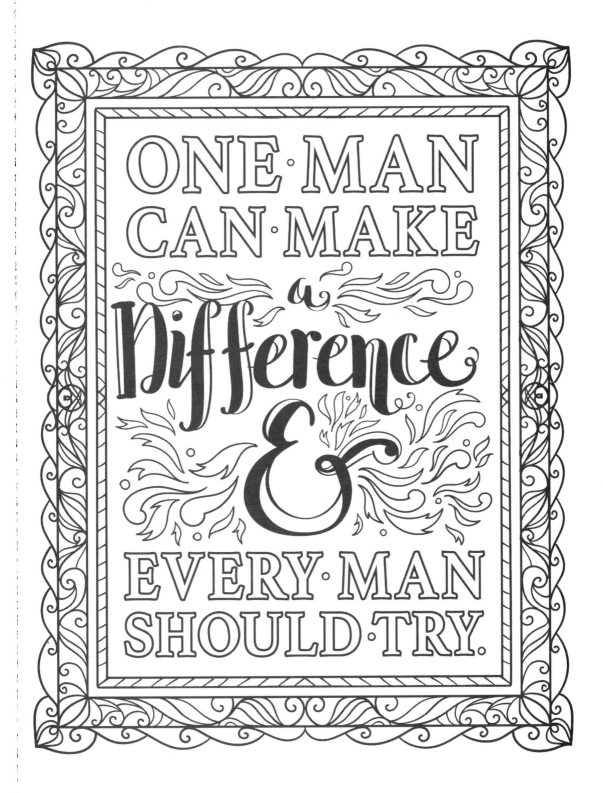

Men are such a
combination of good and bad.

Even
though people
may be well known,
they hold in their hearts
the emotions of a simple
person for the moments that
are the most important of
those we know on earth:
birth, marriage
and death.

If you cut people off from what nourishes them spiritually, something in them dies.

If you bungle raising your children, I don't think whatever else you do matters very much.

Dreaming through September
Just a million lovely things
I always will remember.
—FROM "THOUGHTS," A POEM

O—to live by the sea is my only wish.

—FROM "SEA JOY," A POEM

The greatest responsibility is your children. If my children
turned out badly, I'd feel that nothing I had done was worthwhile.

The river of sludge
will go on and on.
It isn't about me.

A camel makes an elephant feel like a jet plane.

Maybe I'm just dazzled and picture myself in a
glittering world of crowned heads and Men of Destiny.

I love walking on the angry shore, To watch the angry sea;
Where summer people were before, But now there's only me.
—FROM "THOUGHTS," A POEM

There are two kinds of women;
those who want power in the world
and those who want power in bed.

Everywhere, peace is uppermost in
women's minds...if we can't keep the peace,
then the other issues aren't important.

The children have been a
wonderful gift to me, and I'm thankful to have
once again seen our world through their eyes.

...bushels, barrels, carts
and lorry loads of
love to you.

I am happiest when I am alone.

SHE SAID IT BEST

Jackie Kennedy Onassis